# Canterbury to Rome Via Lourdes

A Joyful Pilgrimage from Episcopal Clergyman to Catholic Convert

*"To live is to change…"*

Saint John Henry Newman

# Dedication

"To two princes of the Church whose charism
brings me closer to Christ."

*Saint John Henry Newman and
His Eminence Timothy Cardinal Dolan*

# TABLE OF CONTENTS

# A JOYFUL PILGRIM

# CANTERBURY TO ROME VIA LOURDES

From an early age, I knew I had a vocation—an undefined calling to serve God and his people. After three decades of devoted service in the Episcopal Church, I made a profound decision. In April, His Eminence, Cardinal Dolan, welcomed me into the Roman Catholic Church at St. Patrick's Cathedral in New York during the Easter Vigil. This personal letter's subjects are the how and why of this change, the faith journey that led me here, and the path ahead. It's my way of sharing my story with those considering conversion to the Catholic Church, those struggling with their faith, and all who can find inspiration in the joy of my homecoming.

When I ramble in this narrative, please bear with me. It appropriately reflects my wandering path to conversion to the Catholic Faith. The paths were not straight. The destination was not noticeable. But in the words of Saint Paul, while I viewed through a glass darkly, what I saw in that proverbial mirror was an image of God calling me closer to Him. And I heard a voice telling me to keep asking, looking, and praying for the light to lead me home.

## SOLID PROTESTANT STOCK

I was born into "solid Protestant stock," with Episcopalian and Quaker parents, in the White-Anglo-Saxon-Protestant capital of America: Darien, Connecticut. I will leave sketches of my family background and growing up for later. Instead, let us jump forward to the operative events of this narrative—my ordination, life as an Episcopal priest, and embracing the Catholic faith.

In 1992, Bishop Walmsley of the Episcopal Diocese of Connecticut ordained me as a deacon. I then served parishes in Tennessee, New York City, Long Island, Connecticut, and North Carolina. I have served as a transitional deacon, assistant pastor, visiting clergy, interim priest, vicar, and diocesan staffer. And while I rapidly evolved in my ministry, so did the Episcopal Church . . . taking on an increasingly partisan commitment to progressive politics and social causes. I'll not dwell on what I saw as an increasingly secular and trendy social colorization of the Episcopal Church. Those trends are only tangential to my conversion, which was one of attraction to Catholicism, not rejection of Anglicanism.

My call to ministry came relatively early in my life. When ordained as a deacon, I saw myself embarking on a lifetime of service, intensely devoted to serving Christ through the people, places, and events I encountered daily. My passion for helping those in need, particularly those with developmental disabilities, led me to serve on a family foundation, owning and operating several group homes in the wider Palm Beach area. My service at various Episcopal parishes, notably at St. Thomas Fifth Avenue and St. John's Salisbury, Connecticut, shaped my vision of what Christian ministry could be.

Reflecting on my years in Episcopal ministry has always been satisfying. But yet, I felt something was missing. Still, I am humbly grateful for the opportunity to serve, the wonderful parish families that welcomed me, and the fantastic experiences that shaped me in many ways. I will always treasure my memories and lessons from the saintly clergy colleagues I was blessed to serve. Their example will always be part of my identity.

## THERE MUST BE "MORE"

*Pictured: L-R: David Sellery, Fr. Thomas Coogan, Jane Sellery at St. Patrick's, Bayshore, New York*

Despite the goodwill and the satisfaction I experienced, I felt a constant void that I could not express, much less fill. Increasingly, I had the sense that there must be more. My understanding of what that "more" might be grew from my close friendship with Monsignor Tom Coogan, then pastor of St. Patrick's Catholic Church in Bayshore Long Island. My church, St. Peter's Episcopal in Bayshore, was only about a mile from Monsignor Tom's Church. We were both about the same age. We both managed extensive plants and parish schools. But somehow, I envied Monsignor Tom for some undefined asset he had, and I wanted but couldn't articulate. It all seems obvious in my conversion, but I finally took the gift of faith to see it.

My fellow convert, Saint John Henry Cardinal Newman, captured the "more" I was looking for in the transcendent spiritual energy of the Catholic Church: *"It is the Great Presence which makes a Catholic Church different from every other place in the world. It is as no other place can be . . . holy."*

A defining miraculous moment in my faith journey came at a place where miracles abound—in Lourdes, where the healing grace of God is palpable in the air, in the waters, and in the pilgrims. Lourdes profoundly affected me, deepening my sense of the divine and beckoning me to express my faith entirely.

The sacramental gatherings I attended in Lourdes and later at Champion, Wisconsin, with the Order of Malta opened my eyes to the missing pieces of spiritual life I had sought for years. Not knowing what to expect, I felt myself being drawn reluctantly but joyfully onward into communion with the one, holy, Apostolic faith of Jesus Christ. Finally, St. Augustine's words resonated in me: *"Our hearts are restless until they rest in you."*

## LOURDES, NOT DAMASCUS; LOVE, NOT LIGHTNING

Pictured: David Sellery in Lourdes

My pilgrimage to Lourdes with the Order of Malta was profoundly transformative. As a novice pilgrim, I had high expectations. Still, nothing prepared me for sharing the healing joy with my fellow pilgrims, the sacred sense of peace that permeates that holy ground, and the palpable presence of Christ's love that I encountered at every turn. That experience deepened my commitment to the power of prayer and introduced me to a greater understanding of the sacraments, which continue to guide my faith journey today.

At Lourdes, I experienced what Cardinal Dolan describes as prayer's transformational power: *"Prayer immediately turns us into something greater than ourselves."* What is even more astounding is that the power of prayer is infinite—there are no blackouts or short circuits. Every day, every hour, every minute, Christ's presence in worship is at our call.

If you had told me ten years ago that I would travel to the foothills of the Pyrenees to experience my miracle, I don't know whether I would have greeted the news with a polite smile, a shake of the head, or, most likely, a less than polite sneer. I know I would never have said,

"Thank you. This fills the hole in my soul I have been trying to fill for years." Unlike Saint Paul, my conversion was not shocking. It was sublime. I was not blinded by lightning. I was surrounded by love, elevated by hope, and anchored in newfound faith.

## EMBRACING GOD'S GLORIOUS MYSTERIES

The power of prayer and communion with Christ in the Mass now shapes my journey. Many evangelical Protestant denominations have claimed proprietorship of enabling direct contact with God without what they view as the interference of clergy.

On the contrary, in communion with the real presence of Christ in the Eucharist, I am one with my Savior. He in me, and I in Him. I have a unique contact with God, a way to communicate my deepest hopes, fears, and gratitude.

Also, I have discovered that the structure and rhythm of daily prayer, especially the Rosary, is an integral part of my spiritual life. The Rosary holds a revered place in my life. It is a source of strength and serenity, a way to connect deeply with the mysteries of Christ's life and the joys, sorrows, and glorification of Mary. Participating in the "live Rosary prayers" hosted by the Order of Malta every Sunday evening has become a cherished part of my routine. It completes my prayer life and strengthens my faith.

For over 25 years, I have prayed the Roman Breviary daily. This practice has fundamentally shaped my prayer life, providing a consistent rhythm of prayer and reflection that has anchored me in imitation of Christ. The daily recitation of the Divine Office, especially the Office of Readings, which includes writings from early patristic writers, has been a source of strength and guidance, drawing me closer to God and deepening my faith.

As the gospel tells us, our gift of faith is not meant to be hoarded. We must actively give it away, share it, and celebrate it. My work as a writer has been integral to my spiritual life. Through my website, davidsellery.org, I provided weekly commentary on the upcoming Sunday texts. This work was fed by daily prayer, with a particular focus on the Office of Readings from the Breviary. The insights from early Church Fathers and other patristic writers enriched my reflections and deepened my understanding of the Scripture.

In conversion, I have reflected on St. John Paul II's words in his Apostolic Letter, Rosarium Virginis Mariae: "The repetition of the Hail Mary in the Rosary gives us a share in God's own wonder and pleasure. In jubilant amazement, we acknowledge the greatest miracle of history." Understanding the Rosary's power deepened my appreciation for its role in my spiritual journey.

The Mass plays a central role in my faith. It is the source and summit of Christian life. It is where we encounter Christ. It is where we consume him in the Eucharist, where His Body and Blood nourish us, transform us, and become part of us. My daily participation in the Mass has become a growing affirmation of my faith, deepening my connection to the Church and its teachings. As if speaking specifically for me, Cardinal Newman prayed, "O most sacred, loving heart of Jesus, thou art concealed in the Holy Eucharist. In worshiping thee, I worship my incarnate God, my Emanuel.

## MORAL BEACONS

In my conversion, like that of Cardinal Newman, I am not rejecting my family roots, my years of Anglican service, or my devoted clergy colleagues. Instead, I have been drawn to the faith that preceded all their lifetimes.

In that light, I love, understand, and appreciate them more and wish I could share the joy I have found in the Catholic Church.

My late grandmother, Mrs. Elizabeth Chapman Forster, was and continues to be a tremendous moral beacon in my life. She is a blue-blood descendant from multiple Mayflower families.

Pictured: Elizabeth Chapman Forster

"Boo," as she has been affectionately known since childhood, was a model of old New England rectitude, now found mainly in novels. Despite that, she was fun. She was an athlete, adventurer, and voracious reader with an inquisitive mind, and she instinctively imprinted Christian virtues on her entire family.

She was a winner, and we all aspired to emulate her. To do that, we had to be thoroughly honest, instinctively kind and polite, charitable, dutiful, modest, and industrious. In short, we were to embody the whole catalog of virtues described as the ideal Protestant ethic.

Her guidance insulated me against peer pressure and instilled values that guide my spiritual life to this day. Boo has always been a tremendous spiritual example in my life. Her integrity, goodness, and commitment to Christian character profoundly shaped my call to ministry. In her view, we knew we should stick with the winners.

And that is what I was doing forty-two years ago, working as a summer youth intern in a local church camp alongside my high school classmate, Richard Reeves. Suddenly, our idyllic summer was tragically interrupted. Somehow, Richard had contracted a rare, virulent blood condition, and all the resources of Yale Medical Center couldn't save him.

Into the horror, pain, and confusion of that summer walked another moral beacon, the Reverend Mark Orr. He brought the peace of the risen Christ to Richard in his last days. He comforted Richard's family through shock, grief, and rage. He counseled us kids through our turmoil of sorrow, confusion, and fear. Mark Orr was everywhere, and everywhere he went, things got better. That life of blessed healing is what I wanted. And that call logically led me to pursue a vocation as an Episcopal priest.

While at the seminary in New York City, I interned at The Church of St. Mary the Virgin and worked at Safe Space Shelter. These experiences,

in the epicenter of drug and sex trafficking, deepened my resolve to serve and uplift those in need. While I cannot measure the good I did. These experiences gave me a fair accounting and a lasting impression of the immediate wages of sin. I knew I was called to take the peace of Christ out of my cloistered heart and into the world.

Pictured: Chapel Tower at the General Theological Seminary, New York City

One of my most formative experiences was my work with The HealthCare Chaplaincy under Father Walter Smith SJ is an inspired spiritual entrepreneur, a prodigious scholar, and a good priest. His focus on the single hospital bed, one person at a time in crisis seeking spiritual solace, taught me the importance of individualized ministry.

More precisely, I had the opportunity to work every day with an organizational wizard, Father Walter Smith, SJ, who took a small struggling charity and transformed it into a spiritual powerhouse serving the major hospitals in the New York area. Father Smith is one of those rare individuals who can seamlessly sprinkle a conversation with quotes from a multiplicity of sources— biblical, literary, scientific— all in context, without strain or affectation.

The Healthcare Chaplaincy succeeded because Father Smith never forgot that with all the financial and administrative distractions of a booming enterprise, his focus is on the single hospital bed, one person at a time in crisis is seeking spiritual solace. In following his example, I have always tried to make the focus of my ministry the single individual or family who comes to the church in need of reconciliation, spiritual direction, practical get-it-done advice, or material support. No matter what else is on your plate, ministry is a one-on-one, heart-to-heart relationship.

I took that example into the pulpit during parish service. In preaching, I try to talk to each beloved brother and sister, not to address an amorphous congregation.

*Pictured: L-R: David Sellery, Bishop Grien, Richard Alton, Wendell Welch, St. Thomas Church Fifth Avenue, New York City*

Another great learning experience was my assignment at St. Thomas, Fifth Avenue, in New York City. It was like being called up from the minor leagues to pitch for the Yankees in the World Series. St. Thomas was an Episcopal ecclesiastical all-star team.

The rector, Father John Andrew, was a brilliant preacher with a significant following who expected his curates to keep pace. While I missed the mark more often than not, it was a tremendous experience to study under an inspired messenger who raised the tone of every aspect of the liturgy and the level of our self-expectation by his mere presence.

While he never used the term, Father Andrew projected "excellence." In his eyes, it was what we owed to God. Father Andrew expected it. And he got it. He was dedicated to the simple majesty of the

Episcopal tradition: perfection in the use of the English language in preaching and proclaiming the glory of God, faithful adherence to the liturgy, masterful performance by the choir, and, most importantly, actively encouraging the congregation to make their own connection with Christ.

I have been blessed with other great mentors and various ministry experiences. But I believe that a deep understanding and complete acceptance most bless me and that what I have called "my ministry" indeed does not belong to me; it is a magnificent gift entrusted by God to be developed and nurtured every day. It is a profound charge to enthusiastically devote my life to sharing God's good news with individuals, families, congregations, and communities to instinctively draw my brothers and sisters together in the body of Christ.

## SERVING CHRIST IN THE MOMENT

*Pictured: St. John's Cold Spring Harbor, Cold Spring Harbor, New York*

As an "interim rector" at St. John's in Cold Spring Harbor, I witnessed the ebbs and flows of parish life, gradually growing the congregation and strengthening community ties. I was blessed with great mentors and a wide variety of ministry experiences. But I felt most blessed by the warm acceptance of the parish family and their confident expectation that I was there to bring them closer to Christ. From my Episcopal seminary days, I have known and honored the "interim rector" tradition as a bridge to serve and stabilize the congregation as they plan for succession and continuation of parish leadership. While I had served as "visiting clergy," this was my first experience as an "interim."

And I confess that while I understood and have embraced the concept and role, I've never been entirely comfortable with the formulation "interim rector." I suppose it's because the title conveys a certain logical and emotional dissonance, akin to *pater en passant* or transient shepherd.

In prayer and reflection, I have realized what a great lesson it is to live with the qualifying modifier "interim" attached to your identity. Indeed, we are all ultimately "interims." This world is not our home. You and I are only on a temporary assignment. We were created for something infinitely better. How we deal with that irrefutable fact determines how we spend our "interim" here on earth and how we will spend our eternity.

As fellow Christian "interims" here on this earth, God expects us all to live in the moment, but not for the moment. Living in nostalgic fantasy or recrimination diverts us from the reality of witnessing Christ's love in the here and now. Living in projection is an equally invidious distraction. We are tempted to push the tough choices down the road or look right past the immediate opportunities God gives us daily to listen, be considerate, and help.

But the most tragic and ubiquitous variation is the temptation to live in the moment and for the moment. It's not just about carpe diem ("seizing the day"). It is also about edi diem ("devouring the day"), shoveling more stuff into the hole in our souls, buying and consuming immediate happiness, and experiencing the fleeting endorphin rush of well-being. Sometimes sooner, but most certainly later, we learn that trying to have it all in the here and now is a no-win game. Time, life, fortune, favor, and health are all interim gifts. Only God's love and the gifts that grow from it endures.

Our time here is so brief. God wants us to use it to love Him and serve Him by loving and serving each other. The time I spend fretting or recriminating is wasted. God doesn't care about our crisis du jour. But He does care if we take all that life serves up and use it as a continuum of opportunities to witness His love for each other.

So, as one "interim" to another, we praise God for bringing us together in His love. We confidently seek His plan for us in all of life's twists and turns. We face the day with the courage to act in the moment— the only moment we have — to fulfill our pledge that: *"Thy will be done on earth, as it is heaven."*

## NEW BEACONS FOR NEW ROADS

As I have tried to explain, throughout my life's pilgrimage, I have been blessed to be guided by great moral beacons — Granny Boo, Reverend Orr, Father Smith, Father Andrew — but I believe that the most significant moral beacon of all, most blessed and most guides me our Lord and Savior Jesus Christ, calling me to see his living image in those in need of spiritual and physical nourishment. So, what I have called "my ministry" does not belong to me. It is a response to a vocational call, a magnificent gift entrusted by God to be developed and nurtured daily. It is a profound charge to enthusiastically devote my life to sharing God's good news with individuals, families, congregations, and communities to draw my brothers and sisters together in the body of Christ.

At Lourdes, I saw the healing power of our faith. I also saw that a unique gift to do great good at a time of great need resided in a vocation to the priesthood. I know that this is what I have always wanted to do. I know I want to be a priest.

That is where God is calling me today. I love the life of a priest—everything about it. I celebrate the beauty of the liturgy. I look to the guidance of scripture. I answer the gospel imperative to serve. I remain in constant awe of the healing power of faith in ordinary people's everyday lives.

God has a plan for me. He is calling me to witness Christ's love in the world as an open priest to Him and sees in my vocation an opportunity for effective leadership and productive partnership in our faith journey.

I was blessed through all those years of service in the Episcopal Church. But with all that affectionately recalled, I return to Saint John Henry Newman's judgment: "To be deep in history is to cease to be Protestant." With love and respect for my Protestant family and friends, I found a resonance I never could see as an Anglican in Catholic tradition's depth, beauty, and fullness.

As the road to Rome opened, I have been guided by powerful new beacons, including His Eminence Cardinal Dolan and His Excellency Bishop Edmund Whalen. Encouraged by their support and that of my wife, Jane, I took the most significant step in my pilgrimage.

Pictured: *David and Jane during the Pilgrimage for Life at the Sisters of Life Retreat House, Washington, DC*

Jane and I are now affiliate members of the Order of Malta, the American Association, whose support has been invaluable. Jane, a professional family counselor and social worker, will travel to Lourdes this summer to serve the medically fragile pilgrims and their families. Our younger son, William, aged 16, is committed to the youth pilgrimage to Lourdes. He attended last year with Our Lady's Pilgrimage and intends to make a lifelong commitment to the Hospitalité in Lourdes.

My commitment to serving others is unwavering. This change in my life, my resigning from Episcopal orders, does not mean stepping back from an active life of service. Instead, as an ardent Catholic communicant in my active life, God is calling me to the priesthood in the holy Apostolic faith, which was never more immediate, compelling, and persistent.

Reflecting on Pope Francis' words, "To change is to become more like Christ," I look to my coming home to the Catholic Church as an invitation to finally answer my calling since childhood— now in complete imitation of Christ.

Today, I focus on continuing my daily growth, renewing my relationship with God each morning, and keeping my faith fresh while looking for opportunities to share the good news. Perhaps it's because I'm still relatively young and energetic, or I am predisposed to see each new turn in my ministry as a new adventure with Christ.

Whatever the reason, I feel God's call to serve him is stronger than ever. I hear a clear vocational call to the priesthood in the Catholic Church.

## A 21ST CENTURY VOCATION IN AN APOSTOLIC CHURCH

What a unique role we have, living in the twenty-first century's Artificial Intelligence (AI) world and yet hearing a timeless vocational call across the centuries to an Apostolic priesthood. Our role is not a paradox but a testament to the enduring relevance of our mission.

Pundits have labeled it, clinicians have diagnosed it, and philosophers have decried it. They call it "The Shock of the New on Steroids, Mega Sensory Overload, The Accelerating Constancy of Change." It all adds to the same thing: a pressing need to do too much in too little time.

By definition, the mix of "too little" and "too much" is a surefire formula for failure. We all cope with it. On occasion, most of us succumb to the legion of "could have, would have, should have" events and subsequent recriminations.

Clergy are no exception. They engaged in a recurring struggle to address conflicting imperatives, victims of the daily triage of tasks, and sorting out what to do when there is too much to do.

Then there is the emotional whiplash of conducting a funeral, a wedding, and a christening one weekend and meeting with the parish or community leadership at breakfast the following day to tackle an administrative challenge or an emergency charitable need. Through it all, there is a temptation to grow a protective layer of bark or to hold back on involvement. That is when, in prayer, I am reminded that the task is not mine alone, but Christ's who lives within me.

Ministerial, emotional, and administrative "multitasking" is an increasing requisite for an influential priest. With it, there is a constant danger of succumbing to sensory overload by falling back on routine formulas to limit emotional exposure and preserve energy. There is also the temptation to shortcut someone coming to you with their concerns by projecting your answer rather than hearing them out and helping them with the discovery process that leads them satisfactorily to their answer, not yours. Again, most of the time, with God's help, I take time to listen. And together, we get it right.

I have been blessed with excellent health and a high energy level. I live with the model of Christ to help me connect, not with congregants as clients or customers, but with my brothers and sisters in Christ, whose minister I was and hope to be again. That means, despite distractions, being fully engaged in the moment and helping each grow in their faith.

One distraction from living in the priestly moment has been my unabashed love of administration. Maybe it's a hangover from my professional management experience. Perhaps it's an inherent predisposition. But I must tell myself to stop playing with the pie charts and posting the blog and return to prayer. Who knows what guidance we would all have lost if Aquinas, Augustine, or Anselm had laptops? In prayer, I remember that development campaigns and renovations enable the mission. They are not the mission.

I suspect my ongoing challenge is not unlike that of most Christians. We are in the world, but we are not of the world. We must live in the moment but not for the moment. God has bigger plans for us. In that spirit, we must constantly evaluate and prioritize. When in doubt, "What would Jesus do?" is the best rule of thumb I have ever heard.

I pray that with God's help on most days, I will get most of it right: that I will put people ahead of things, that I will take time to listen, and that I will be sensitive to a cry for help or an opportunity to serve, that I will remember that I am only here to do His work and that I will trust in His help and forgiveness to prevent stringing too many bad days together.

All of which brings me back to my first moral beacon, "Granny Boo." She would bridle at being considered pious or profound. But she recently taught us a lesson that my brother reminded me of. On her 90th birthday, looking out over her extended family assembled to honor her, she waxed uncharacteristically philosophical: The growth and development of one's character is seldom pleasant during construction.

But what comfort and joy it is when the foundations are firm, and the roots are deep. Compared to Boo, I still have such a long way to go. My character remains in formation, but I have had the benefit of excellent mentors and role models. I have the constant companionship of the risen Christ. Every day, I long to fully engage in the priestly vocation to which I am called. I look for a congregation to share their experience, hope, and joy as we journey together.

## COMING HOME

*Pictured: L-R: Jane Sellery, His Eminence, Cardinal Timothy Dolan, David Sellery on the occasion of the convalidation of their wedding vows, St Patrick's Cathedral, New York City*

While it took me over fifty years to travel from Canterbury to Rome and from Anglican to Catholic, I'm not home yet; there are miles to go. I hope to travel to them as a priest serving in the Catholic Church.

My transition took an enormous step in a joyful event on March 30th, 2024, when Cardinal Dolan confirmed me at St. Patrick's Cathedral. This event also marked the blessing of my marriage, making it a doubly important milestone. To be confirmed and to have my marriage blessed by Cardinal Dolan at St. Patrick's was a truly glorious experience, a never-hoped-for high point on my long, personal journey of faith. As the Catechism of the Catholic Church states, *"Confirmation perfects Baptismal grace; it is the sacrament which gives the Holy Spirit to root us more deeply in the divine filiation"* (CCC 1316).

## LOOKING BACK, LOOKING FORWARD

I leave the Episcopal Church with gratitude and admiration for my brothers and sisters in Christ who faithfully serve in that tradition. The experiences, grace, and regard I received in the Episcopal community have indelibly marked my spiritual journey. I will always be grateful for the openness and commitment to our shared mission and ministry shown by everyone I worked with during that period. Service in the Catholic faith marks a new chapter in my life. My commitment to helping God's people has been taken up to a higher level, a place I could never have reached before.

The inspired motto of St. Thomas Aquinas: *"Domine nihil nisi te"* ("Lord, nothing except You"), which I adopted at my Episcopal ordination, takes on greater meaning in my new life as a Catholic. I am now more dedicated to a life of prayer and service, continually seeking to follow God's will. The steadfast support from my fellow members of the Order of Malta, my parish priest's guidance, the Mass's transformative power, and a dedicated life of prayer have all been pillars of strength in this journey.

Looking ahead, I am excited about continuing to share my joy of discovery in a new visitor's guidebook, *Journey to Lourdes: A Catholic Pilgrim's Travel Guide*. This book aims to guide and inspire others on their pilgrimages, sharing their profound experiences and spiritual growth.

Presently, I serve Catholic Charities, The Archdiocese of Hartford, as their Senior Director of Fund Development. After serving as Director of Development and Member Engagement for the American Association of the Order of Malta in New York City, where I was instrumental in the association, raising more than $22.4 million. I look forward to bringing my experience and passion for service to this new role, helping to further Catholic Charities' mission of supporting those in need throughout the Archdiocese of Hartford.

All of this is to say that we are here to witness His love in the world. We are here to make a difference—actively helping, sharing, giving, and forgiving—and then getting up the next day and doing it all again. We are committed to walking the walk with Jesus, and He is committed to walking us all the way home. What a joy and pleasure it is to walk in the way of the Lord! *"Master, to whom shall we go? You have the words of eternal life."* John 6:68-69 New American Bible (CCD-USCCB).

## VALEDICTORY

As each of us continues on our pilgrimages of faith —with all their surprises, twists, turns, and pitfalls, their inspirations, and their blessings — I take encouragement from Cardinal Newman's ageless prayer: *"Lead kindly light amid the encircling gloom, lead thou me on."* In humble imitation of Saint John Henry's monumental conversion, my journey from the Episcopal Church to the Roman Catholic faith is a testament to how a deeply committed Christian should always seek and always follow the call for a closer, more accurate, more complete union with Christ. I pray my struggle encourages others to follow Christ in answer to Saint Peter's question: Quo Vadis? For me, after a lifelong pilgrimage, my joyful response is that I am going home to Rome via Lourdes to give my life to Christ, both now and forever.